Don't Fall Victim Identity Theft

How to Protect Your Name from Being Used Without Your Consent

By: Brian Lewis

9781635014310

PUBLISHERS NOTES

Disclaimer – Speedy Publishing LLC

This publication is intended to provide helpful and informative material. It is not intended to diagnose, treat, cure, or prevent any health problem or condition, nor is intended to replace the advice of a physician. No action should be taken solely on the contents of this book. Always consult your physician or qualified health-care professional on any matters regarding your health and before adopting any suggestions in this book or drawing inferences from it.

The author and publisher specifically disclaim all responsibility for any liability, loss or risk, personal or otherwise, which is incurred as a consequence, directly or indirectly, from the use or application of any contents of this book.

Any and all product names referenced within this book are the trademarks of their respective owners. None of these owners have sponsored, authorized, endorsed, or approved this book.

Always read all information provided by the manufacturers' product labels before using their products. The author and publisher are not responsible for claims made by manufacturers.

This book was originally printed before 2014. This is an adapted reprint by Speedy Publishing LLC with newly updated content designed to help readers with much more accurate and timely information and data.

Speedy Publishing LLC

40 E Main Street, Newark, Delaware, 19711

Contact Us: 1-888-248-4521

Website: http://www.speedypublishing.co

REPRINTED Paperback Edition: 9781635014310:

Manufactured in the United States of America

DEDICATION

This book is dedicated to my best friend, Mary. Ever since we were children, you've always had my back. I will always treasure you and our friendship.

TABLE OF CONTENTS

Chapter 1- Identifying Identity Theft...5

Chapter 2- How Internet Use Increases the Chances of Identity Theft...12

Chapter 3- Proving Your Identity When You're Already a Victim 16

Chapter 4- How to Resolve Specific Cases of Identity Theft.........23

Chapter 5- How to Re-Establish Your Credit Score.........................32

Chapter 6- Sample Dispute Letters...35

Chapter 7- Protecting Yourself from Identity Thieves 48

Chapter 8- Internet Security Tips for You and Your Family.........52

About The Author...59

CHAPTER 1- IDENTIFYING IDENTITY THEFT

It's more than a simple impersonation of someone. You've heard of people impersonating a police officer, or the girl who claimed to be Jessica Simpson's personal assistant and securing thousands of dollars of items she used for herself. Identity theft is a crime that occurs – usually without attaching a face to a name – until the criminal is caught.

Identity theft occurs when your personal information is stolen and used without your knowledge to commit fraud or other crimes. a con artist appropriates another's name, address, Social Security number or other identifying information and uses that information to open new credit card accounts, take over existing accounts, obtain loans in the victim's name or steal funds from the victim's checking, savings, or investment accounts. "Identity theft" is technically defined as the use, transfer or theft of personal identifying information for the purpose of committing a crime.

Federal law prevents identity theft victims from being held liable for bills incurred by imposters. Consumers, however, can spend months, and even years, in repairing the damage to their good credit. Businesses are affected greatly as well by this crime. They have given out goods and services with illegally obtained credit cards. With credit protection, as long as the victim can prove they didn't make the purchases, these businesses must write off the bill without recovering the merchandise.

A similar crime is identity fraud. A variety of abuses of the bankruptcy system, including the concealment of assets in bankruptcy, the making of false sworn financial statements in bankruptcy proceedings, and the filing of bankruptcies under false social security numbers are often dubbed "identity fraud" by prosecutors and government regulators. Cons attempt to obtain the benefits of bankruptcy such as relief from debt collection, while attempting to escape negative credit consequences. In one case they leased a residence and obtained credit with the name and social security number of an unsuspecting victim then they occupied the residence, ran up the credit cards, and then filed for bankruptcy in the victim's name. One bankruptcy petition was filed in the name of a recently deceased father. Such fraudulent bankruptcy filings often wreak havoc on innocent people who must spend substantial resources to clear their credits and their names.

The rampant theft and abuse of other people's credit histories and social security numbers has become one of the biggest problems of consumer bankruptcy fraud. Both crimes have become rampant affecting millions and millions of people in the United States alone. You may think you're protected, but you may be surprised exactly how these criminals get your personal information How Is Your Information Stolen? A lost or stolen wallet is just one way for a thief to get your information. They can fraudulently access your credit report by posing as an employer, loan officer, or landlord. Internet records that are unprotected are another source. Some will go dumpster diving looking for bills or other papers with your personal information on it. Many people receive daily offers for credit cards. If you're not interested, you just throw it away. Thieves love finding these!

The problem of criminals rummaging through bins for such documents is well known and there have been reports of organized gangs paying people to pick through landfill sites for such documents. A change of address form can be used to divert billing statements to another location. This will give them access to your credit card numbers. Shoulder surfing is done at the ATM machine and phone booths. This means the criminal will stand behind you as you enter in your PIN number or phone information. Police have already arrested several individuals copying cards using the cash machines themselves. A small electronic camera is mounted above the keypad of the cash machine and a card reader, often only a few centimeters thick, goes over the card slot. At a busy machine hundreds of card numbers can be collected in a few hours and turned into cloned cards.

The wide availability of small card scanners has also made card skimming a problem. In a matter of seconds your card's magnetic strip can be copied and a crooked employee of a restaurant or retail outlet can copy many cards in a day.

By far the biggest problem with identity theft is 'social engineering': this means someone obtaining information by deception, and usually involves some form of incentive or plain old-fashioned flattery. A veneer of officialdom also oils the wheels and it's a surprisingly effective technique. Several recent experiments have shown that nine in 10 people would give up computer passwords in exchange for a small gift like a chocolate bar when questioned by someone holding a clipboard. All too frequently people give out sensitive information over the telephone when they have no proof that the person at the other end is who they say they are.

While identity theft committed in this manner still accounts for the majority of fraud, security experts are warning that such attacks are increasingly being abandoned in favor of electronic methods. One of the most dangerous methods of identity theft used online is key logging, which bypasses documents altogether. Here a piece of software records every keystroke made on the computer, including all of your log-in details. Such software is generally spread by viruses or as attachments in spam. Email in particular allows personal contact with millions of people at the push of a button and fraudsters have taken advantage of this. It has also allowed for the merging of old and new types of identity theft to create potentially devastating crimes such as phishing. This is another old con in modern form and involves setting up a plausible looking website that claims to be an online business.

It's a cheaper, more anonymous variant of fly-by-night operators setting up stalls in abandoned shops. Visitors are encouraged to input personal information, usually after receiving an email requesting they confirm login details or check the status of an order. Such emails are sent out to millions of addresses and usually contain warnings that action must be taken immediately in order to frighten the recipient into acting without thinking. This is an especially scary way of obtaining your information since most of these e-mails are very, very real looking. The non-educated consumer can easily be taken in by simply clicking on a link and entering in a password. This is especially common for people who have Pay Pal accounts or who sell at online auction sites like eBay.

Web monitoring and hosting companies work hard to shut these websites down within days but they can harvest thousands of account details in that time. Online banks in particular have been targeted but so too have eBay and PayPal. An even more advanced, and harder to detect, form of this con has come to light recently nicknamed pharming. This involves criminals using computer security holes to reprogram computers that allocate the addresses for all web pages so even if you key in the correct web address, your web browser may be directed to a bogus site. Such attacks are technically possible although none have been confirmed as yet.

Are You Already a Victim of Identity Theft?

Unfortunately, the most common way people find out they are victims of identity theft is when the damage is already done. One victim tells the account of how she found out her information had been stolen.

She writes: "I had been thinking about buying a cellular phone but someone beat me to the punch. This person set up an account using his name and paid two bills using my Visa/debit card number. I'm not sure how he got the number since there's only one card. I've heard a lot of theories in the last few days. Nextel allowed this man to set up the account using my card and never verified the information. Had they checked him out, they might have found that the owner of the Visa/debit card was a woman, and not the man starting a cellular phone account. I don't even have a cell phone! The guy took more than half my paycheck, leaving me home all weekend with very little money. Luckily, rent wasn't due."

Yet another victim writes: "On Xxxx xx,2000 - my birthday - my wallet was taken at the checkout counter at (a grocery store). Security cameras showed the checker taking my wallet, and charging nearly $500 of groceries after I left the store. Despite my calling the police, no charges were filed against the individual because he did not "steal" the wallet from my person. The wallet - containing my recently renewed Driver's License, MasterCard, ATM Card, parking card, business cards (with cellular and home numbers), and college ID card (with social security number on it) - was never recovered. The head of store security and the police detective told me that the wallet was probably thrown away." And a third account of identity theft reads: "On September 19, I first became aware that my identity had been stolen. I received a bill from (a department store) - for $675.55 of electronic purchases I did not make. I notified (them), and put fraud alerts at the three credit reporting agencies, and ordered copies of my credit reports. I was dumbfounded by what I discovered: over $7,000 of charges on seven credit cards, with attempts to open 6 more. Starting on September 9th, most accounts had been opened on the Internet. Despite the fraud alert, accounts are still being opened. An account was opened at (a furniture store) on September 22d. The suspect presented my driver's license - and, despite the fraud alert, the miswriting of my social security number, and obvious differences in the signature - was granted instant credit. Subsequently, nearly $3000 in charges was made, in 6 separate instances, over a four-day period."

By the time these people discovered their identity had been stolen, their credit had already been jeopardized and perhaps even ruined. They would have to embark on the unfortunate and long journey of proving their innocence. Though we'll touch on it later in this book, one thing you can do is to monitor your credit reports faithfully. You should also be aware when bills do not arrive as expected or you receive statements for credit cards that you do not have. You may be denied credit for a large purchase and not be given an immediate reason why. This is a HUGE warning sign that your identity may have been compromised – especially if you've always had an excellent credit score.

Finally, if you are receiving phone calls or correspondence from credit reporting agencies or collection departments, you need to look at your credit more closely to see if your information has been breached. These are all warning signs that you should not ignore – under any circumstances! So what do you do if you think you're a victim of identity theft? The first thing you'll need to do is gather important documents and be able to prove your identity.

CHAPTER 2- HOW INTERNET USE INCREASES THE CHANCES OF IDENTITY THEFT

You would hate to think that by ordering that new purse or buying that airline ticket for vacation might end up costing you your identity. While most websites are secure when it comes to transactions, your personal and financial information can be compromised. As a result, they can open credit cards, checking accounts, and even get an ID and purchase a new car with your personal information. As a result, you could end up owing thousands of dollars, as well as have to seek legal help which can cost even more money.

Identify theft can unfortunately happen to anyone. Here is some information that might be helpful in recognizing it and preventing it to maintain your internet security.

Warning Signs to Watch Out For

1. You receive something that you did not order.

2. Unexplained things pop up on your credit report. You might not even notice this until you try to purchase something and you are declined due to your poor credit rating.

3. Unexplained purchases show up in your checking account or on your credit cards.

4. You receive calls from bill collectors for accounts that you did not open.

How to Prevent Identity Theft

1. Always shred any unwanted credit card offers or mail that might contain personal information such as your account number, social security number, checking account number, etc.

2. Stay up to date on the latest scams. There are several websites devoted to this.

3. Use anti-spam ware and ensure that your e-mail account has a spam filter on it to deposit unwanted emails into.

4. Check the privacy policy on a website that asks for personal information. Don't submit anything if it doesn't have one.

5. Don't keep your personal or financial information on your computer. Likewise, don't store your passwords on your computer either.

6. Don't open an attachment if you receive an e-mail from someone that you don't know. Use an anti-virus program to scan the e-mail first to make sure that it doesn't contain any phishing or virus programs on it.

7. Keep your firewalls and anti-virus software up-to-date on all of your computers.

If you suspect that your security has been compromised, change all of your passwords, cancel your credit cards, close your bank account, and report it to the police. Also, report the activity at once to your financial institution and Credit Card Company.

Teen-Focused Attacks on the Internet

Every day you hear about teens being attacked or compromised by people who take advantage of them by using the internet. For a parent, this can be a frightening concept. However, there are measures that you can take to protect your teens on the internet. The following is a list of tips to help ensure internet security for your teens.

1. Talk to your teen. First, make sure that you talk to your teens about internet security. Having good communication is always the most effective preventive measure. After all, you can put security features on your computer at home, but teens have access to computers almost everywhere they go. Make sure that your teen understands the dangers associated conversing with people they don't know on the internet, meeting people off of the internet, and using their financial information to purchase something online.

2. Be aware. There are thousands of chat rooms, message boards, and forums out there for teens. As a result, there are thousands

of people out there who pretend to be teens in order to converse with them. This is a dangerous situation. When your teen is at home, monitor their internet use without being too overbearing. Know what chat rooms they use, what people they converse with on a daily basis, and ask to be able to access their Facebook and Myspace pages. Let them know that if they are going to have a computer in their room you have the right to look at their internet usage from time to time.

3. Report any suspicious behavior. If your teen tells you that someone on the internet wants to meet them, do some investigating yourself on this person. Likewise, if your teen tells you that they are troubled by someone who is contacting them on the internet then report this person to the police. It is better to be safe than sorry.

4. Don't let cyber bullying go unnoticed. Cyber bullying is a very real threat to internet security, as well as physical and emotional well-being to teens. If your teen is being cyber bullied then report the offenders to that website that it is occurring on and then let the school know as well. More and more organizations and websites are taking this seriously these days. On Facebook, if you block someone now, it actually asks you if it was due to cyber bullying.

CHAPTER 3- PROVING YOUR IDENTITY WHEN YOU'RE ALREADY A VICTIM

You might think this would be the easiest part of combating identity theft, but it really isn't. Think about it. The thief was allowed to pose as you, how do the companies know that you're not also just trying to impersonate someone else? Applications or other transaction records related to the theft of your identity may help you prove that you are a victim. For example, you may be able to show that the signature on an application is not yours. These documents also may contain information about the identity thief that is valuable to law enforcement.

By law, companies must give you a copy of the application or other business transaction records relating to your identity theft if you submit your request in writing. Be sure to ask the company representative where you should mail your request. Companies must provide these records at no charge to you within 30 days of receipt of your request and supporting documents. You also may give permission to any law enforcement agency to get these records, or ask in your written request that a copy of these records be sent to a particular law enforcement officer. The company can ask you for proof of your identity. This may be a photocopy of a government-issued ID card, the same type of information the identity thief used to open or access the account, or the type of information the company usually requests from applicants or customers, and a police report and a completed affidavit, which may be an Identity Theft Affidavit or the company's own affidavit. This all, of course, is a daunting process.

There are steps you can take, however, to organize your case and have all the documents you need at hand to combat the theft of your identity.

Completeness and Accuracy of Information is Essential

Accurate and complete records will help you to resolve your identity theft case more quickly. Have a plan when you contact a company. Don't assume that the person you talk to will give you all the information or help you need. Prepare a list of questions to ask the representative, as well as information about your identity theft.

Don't end the call until you're sure you understand everything you've been told. If you need more help, ask to speak to a supervisor. Write down the name of everyone you talk to, what he or she tells you, and the date the conversation occurred. At the end of the book, we'll provide you with a form to plan out your course of action. Follow this course to provide the most accurate and up-to-date information you can. Follow up in writing with all contacts you've made on the phone or in person.

Use certified mail, return receipt requested, so you can document what the company or organization received and when. Keep copies of all correspondence or forms you send. Keep the originals of supporting documents, like police reports and letters to and from creditors; send copies only. Set up a filing system for easy access to your paperwork. Keep old files even if you believe your case is closed. Once resolved, most cases stay resolved, but problems can crop up.

At this point, you can start the tedious task of contacting the companies you need to in order to get the problem cleared up.

Your First Step

If you have become a victim of identity theft, you are going to be embarking on a long and perilous journey that will, no doubt, be extremely frustrating and filled with stress. Unless you want to accept responsibility for what the thieves did to you – and we assume you don't – accepting the fact that this will take some time to unravel is your very first step. You will be talking to a lot of people, copying a lot of documents, and gathering a lot of information.

Patience is essential, so keep that in mind. The first thing to do is contact your bank or financial institution and put them on notice that your personal information has been compromised. You must also contact credit card companies. Close accounts, like credit cards and bank accounts, immediately. When you open new accounts place passwords on them. Avoid using your mother's maiden name, your birth date, the last four digits of your Social Security number (SSN) or your phone number, or a series of consecutive numbers. Call and speak with someone in the security or fraud department of each company. Follow up in writing, and include copies (NOT originals) of supporting documents. It's important to notify credit card companies and banks in writing.

Send your letters by certified mail, return receipt requested, so you can document what the company received and when. Keep a file of your correspondence and enclosures. When you open new accounts, use new Personal Identification Numbers (PINs) and passwords. As we've said, avoid using easily available information like your mother's maiden name, your birth date, the last four digits of your SSN or your phone number, or a series of consecutive numbers. This is extremely important, so it bears repeating.

If the identity thief has made charges or debits on your accounts, or on fraudulently opened accounts, ask the company for the forms to dispute those transactions:

• For charges and debits on existing accounts, ask the representative to send you the company's fraud dispute forms. If the company doesn't have special forms, write a letter to dispute the fraudulent charges or debits. In either case, write to the company at the address given for "billing inquiries," NOT the address for sending your payments.

• For new unauthorized accounts, ask the representative to send you the company's fraud dispute forms. If the company already has reported these accounts or debts on your credit report, dispute this fraudulent information. Once you have resolved your identity theft dispute with the company, ask for a letter stating that the company has closed the disputed accounts and has discharged the fraudulent debts. This letter is your best proof if errors relating to this account reappear on your credit report or you are contacted again about the fraudulent debt. Call the toll-free fraud number of any of the three nationwide consumer reporting companies and place an initial fraud alert on your credit reports. An alert can help stop someone from opening new credit accounts in your name. We have the contact information for the three credit reporting agencies at the end of the book. A note about fraud alerts needs to be inserted here. There are two types of fraud alerts: an initial alert, and an extended alert.

• An initial alert stays on your credit report for at least 90 days. You may ask that an initial fraud alert be placed on your credit report if you suspect you have been, or are about to be, a victim of identity theft. An initial alert is appropriate if your wallet has been stolen or if you've been taken in by a "phishing" scam. When you place an initial fraud alert on your credit report, you're entitled to one free credit report from each of the three nationwide consumer reporting companies.

• An extended alert stays on your credit report for seven years. You can have an extended alert placed on your credit report if you've been a victim of identity theft and you provide the consumer reporting company with an "identity theft report." When you place an extended alert on your credit report, you're entitled to two free credit reports within twelve months from each of the three nationwide consumer reporting companies. In addition, the consumer reporting companies will remove your name from marketing lists for pre-screened credit offers for five years unless you ask them to put your name back on the list before then. To place either of these alerts on your credit report, or to have them removed, you will be required to provide appropriate proof of your identity: that may include your SSN, name, address and other personal information requested by the consumer reporting company. When a business sees the alert on your credit report, they must verify your identity before issuing you credit. As part of this verification process, the business may try to contact you directly. This may cause some delays if you're trying to obtain credit. To compensate for possible delays, you may wish to include a cell phone number, where you can be reached easily, in your alert. Remember to keep all contact information in your alert current.

Once you place the fraud alert in your file, you're entitled to order free copies of your credit reports, and, if you ask, only the last four digits of your SSN will appear on your credit reports. Once you get your credit reports, review them carefully. Look for inquiries from companies you haven't contacted, accounts you didn't open, and debts on your accounts that you can't explain. Check that information, like your SSN, address/es, name or initials, and employers are correct. If you find fraudulent or inaccurate information, get it removed. Continue to check your credit reports periodically, especially for the first year after you discover the identity theft, to make sure no new fraudulent activity has occurred. When it comes to your driver's license or government issued identification, contact the agency that issued the license or other identification document. Follow its procedures to cancel the document and to get a replacement. Ask the agency to flag your file so that no one else can get a license or any other identification document from them in your name.

If your information has been misused, file a report about the theft with the police, and file a complaint with the Federal Trade Commission, as well. If another crime was committed for example, if your purse or wallet was stolen or your house or car was broken into report it to the police immediately. In all cases of identity theft or fraud, you will be doubly covered by reporting it to the police. They will take a report documenting the crime. After you file the police report, get a copy of it or at the very least, the reference number of the report. It can help you deal with creditors who need proof of the crime. If the police are reluctant to take your report, ask to file a "Miscellaneous Incidents" report, or try another jurisdiction, like your state police. You also can check with your state Attorney General's office to find out if state law requires the police to take reports for identity theft. Check the Blue Pages of your telephone directory for the phone number or look for a list of state Attorneys General.

As far as the FTC is concerned, by sharing your identity theft complaint with the FTC, you will provide important information that can help law enforcement officials across the nation track down identity thieves and stop them. The FTC can refer victims' complaints to other government agencies and companies for further action, as well as investigate companies for violations of laws the agency enforces. You can file a complaint online. If you don't have Internet access, call the FTC's Identity Theft Hotline, toll-free: 1-877- IDTHEFT (438-4338); TTY: 1-866-653- 4261; or write: Identity Theft Clearinghouse, Federal Trade Commission, 600 Pennsylvania Avenue, NW, Washington, DC 20580. Be sure to call the Hotline to update your complaint if you have any additional information or problems. Once you've made these initial steps, there are some specific things that must be done with specific situations.

Chapter 4- How to Resolve Specific Cases of Identity Theft

Because the thief has gained access to your personal information, it's a good idea to protect everything that has to do with your financial information. Some of this information has been touched on previously, but it all bears repeating.

Bank Accounts and Electronic Withdrawals

Different laws determine your legal remedies based on the type of bank fraud you have suffered. For example, state laws protect you against fraud committed by a thief using paper documents, like stolen or counterfeit checks. But if the thief used an electronic fund transfer, federal law applies. Many transactions may seem to be processed electronically but are still considered "paper" transactions. If you're not sure what type of transaction the thief used to commit the fraud, ask the financial institution that processed the transaction.

The Electronic Fund Transfer Act provides consumer protections for transactions involving an ATM or debit card, or another electronic way to debit or credit an account. It also limits your liability for unauthorized electronic fund transfers. You have 60 days from the date your bank account statement is sent to you to report in writing any money withdrawn from your account without your permission. This includes instances when your ATM or debit card is "skimmed" that is, when a thief captures your account number and PIN without your card having been lost or stolen. If your ATM or debit card is lost or stolen, report it immediately because the amount you can be held responsible for depends on how quickly you report the loss.

If you report the loss within two business days of discovery, your personal loss is limited to $50. If you report the loss or theft after two business days, but within 60 days after the unauthorized electronic fund transfer appears on your statement, you could lose up to $500 of what the thief withdraws. If you wait more than 60 days to report the loss or theft, you could lose all the money that was taken from your account after the end of the 60 days. VISA and MasterCard have voluntarily agreed to limit consumers' liability for unauthorized use of their debit cards in most instances to $50 per card, no matter how much time has elapsed since the discovery of the loss or theft of the card.

The best way to protect yourself in the event of an error or fraudulent transaction is to call the financial institution and follow up in writing by certified letter, return receipt requested so you can prove when the institution received your letter. Keep a copy of the letter you send for your records. After receiving your notification about an error on your statement, the institution generally has 10 business days to investigate. The institution must tell you the results of its investigation within three business days after completing it and must correct an error within one business day after determining that it occurred. If the institution needs more time, it may take up to 45 days to complete the investigation but only if the money in dispute is returned to your account and you are notified promptly of the credit. At the end of the investigation, if no error has been found, the institution may take the money back if it sends you a written explanation. In general, if an identity thief steals your checks or counterfeits checks from your existing bank account, stop payment, close the account, and ask your bank to notify Chex Systems, Inc. or the check verification service with which it does business. That way, retailers can be notified not to accept these checks.

While no federal law limits your losses if someone uses your checks with a forged signature, or uses another type of "paper" transaction such as a demand draft, state laws may protect you. Most states hold the bank responsible for losses from such transactions. At the same time, most states require you to take reasonable care of your account. For example, you may be held responsible for the forgery if you fail to notify the bank in a timely manner that a check was lost or stolen. Contact your state banking or consumer protection agency for more information. You can contact major check verification companies directly.

To request that they notify retailers who use their databases not to accept your checks, call: TeleCheck at 1-800-710-9898 or 1-800-927-0188 Certegy, Inc. (previously Equifax Check Systems) at 1-800-437-5120 To find out if the identity thief has been passing bad checks in your name, call: SCAN: 1-800-262-7771 If your checks are rejected by a merchant, it may be because an identity thief is using the Magnetic Information Character Recognition (MICR) code (the numbers at the bottom of checks), your driver's license number, or another identification number. The merchant who rejects your check should give you its check verification company contact information so you can find out what information the thief is using. If you find that the thief is using your MICR code, ask your bank to close your checking account, and open a new one. If you discover that the thief is using your driver's license number or some other identification number, work with your DMV or other identification issuing agency to get new identification with new numbers.

Once you have taken the appropriate steps, your checks should be accepted. The check verification company may or may not remove the information about the MICR code or the driver's license/identification number from its database because this information may help prevent the thief from continuing to commit fraud. If the checks are being passed on a new account, contact the bank to close the account. Also contact Chex Systems, Inc., to review your consumer report to make sure that no other bank accounts have been opened in your name. Dispute any bad checks passed in your name with merchants so they don't start any collections actions against you.

Fraudulent New Accounts

If you have trouble opening a new checking account, it may be because an identity thief has been opening accounts in your name. Chex Systems, Inc. produces consumer reports specifically about checking accounts, and as a consumer reporting company, is subject to the Fair Credit Reporting Act. You can request a free copy of your consumer report by contacting Chex Systems, Inc. If you find inaccurate information on your consumer report, follow the procedures under Correcting Credit Reports to dispute it. Contact each of the banks where account inquiries were made, too. This will help ensure that any fraudulently opened accounts are closed. Bankruptcy Fraud. If you believe someone has filed for bankruptcy in your name, then you need to write to the U.S. Trustee in the region where the bankruptcy was filed. Lists of the U.S. Trustee Programs' Regional Offices are available on the UST website or check the Blue Pages of your phone book under U.S. Government Bankruptcy Administration. In your letter, describe the situation and provide proof of your identity.

The U.S. Trustee will make a criminal referral to law enforcement authorities if you provide appropriate documentation to substantiate your claim. You also may want to file a complaint with the U.S. Attorney and/or the FBI in the city where the bankruptcy was filed. The U.S. Trustee does not provide legal representation, legal advice, or referrals to lawyers. That means you may need to hire an attorney to help convince the bankruptcy court that the filing is fraudulent. The U.S. Trustee does not provide consumers with copies of court documents. You can get them from the bankruptcy clerk's office for a fee. Credit Cards The Fair Credit Billing Act establishes procedures for resolving billing errors on your credit card accounts, including fraudulent charges on your accounts. The law also limits your liability for unauthorized credit card charges to $50 per card. To take advantage of the law's consumer protections, you must: • Write to the creditor at the address given for "billing inquiries," NOT the address for sending your payments. Include your name, address, account number, and a description of the billing error, including the amount and date of the error.

Send your letter so that it reaches the creditor within 60 days after the first bill containing the error was mailed to you. If an identity thief changed the address on your account and you didn't receive the bill, your dispute letter still must reach the creditor within 60 days of when the creditor would have mailed the bill. This is one reason it's essential to keep track of your billing statements, and follow up quickly if your bills don't arrive on time. You should send your letter by certified mail, and request a return receipt. It becomes your proof of the date the creditor received the letter. Include copies (NOT originals) of your police report or other documents that support your position.

Keep a copy of your dispute letter. The creditor must acknowledge your complaint in writing within 30 days after receiving it, unless the problem has been resolved. The creditor must resolve the dispute within two billing cycles (but not more than 90 days) after receiving your letter.

Criminal Violations

Procedures to correct your record within criminal justice databases can vary from state to state, and even from county to county. Some states have enacted laws with special procedures for identity theft victims to follow to clear their names. You should check with the office of your state Attorney General, but you can use the following information as a general guide. If wrongful criminal violations are attributed to your name, contact the police or sheriff's department that originally arrested the person using your identity, or the court agency that issued the warrant for the arrest. File an impersonation report with the police/sheriff's department or the court, and confirm your identity.

Ask the police department to take a full set of your fingerprints, photograph you, and make copies of your photo identification documents, like your driver's license, passport, or travel visa. To establish your innocence, ask the police to compare the prints and photographs with those of the imposter. If the arrest warrant is from a state or county other than where you live, ask your local police department to send the impersonation report to the police department in the jurisdiction where the arrest warrant, traffic citation, or criminal conviction originated. The law enforcement agency should then recall any warrants and issue a "clearance letter" or "certificate of release" (if the thief was arrested or booked). You'll need to keep this document with you at all times in case you're wrongly arrested again. Ask the law enforcement agency to file the record of the follow-up investigation establishing your innocence with the district attorney's (D.A.) office and/or court where the crime took place. This will result in an amended complaint. Once your name is recorded in a criminal database, it's unlikely that it will be completely removed from the official record. Ask that the "key name" or "primary name" be changed from your name to the imposter's name (or to "John Doe" if the imposter's true identity is not known), with your name noted as an alias. You'll also want to clear your name in the court records.

To do this you'll need to determine which state law(s) will help you with this and how. If your state has no formal procedure for clearing your record, contact the D.A.'s office in the county where the case was originally prosecuted. Ask the D.A.'s office for the appropriate court records needed to clear your name. You may need to hire a criminal defense attorney to help you clear your name. You can contact Legal Services in your state or your local bar association for help in finding an attorney. Finally, contact your state Department of Motor Vehicles (DMV) to find out if your driver's license is being used by the identity thief. Ask that your files be flagged for possible fraud.

Stopping Debt Collectors

The Fair Debt Collection Practices Act prohibits debt collectors from using unfair or deceptive practices to collect overdue bills that a creditor has forwarded for collection, even if those bills don't result from identity theft. You can stop a debt collector from contacting you in two ways:

- Write a letter to the collection agency telling them to stop. Once the debt collector receives your letter, the company may not contact you again with two exceptions: They can tell you there will be no further contact, and they can tell you that the debt collector or the creditor intends to take some specific action.

- Send a letter to the collection agency, within 30 days after you received written notice of the debt, telling them that you do not owe the money. Include copies of documents that support your position. Including a copy (NOT original) of your police report may be useful. In this case, a collector can renew collection activities only if it sends you proof of the debt. If you don't have documentation to support your position, be as specific as possible about why the debt collector is mistaken. The debt collector is responsible for sending you proof that you're wrong. For example, if the debt you're disputing originates from a credit card you never applied for; ask for a copy of the application with the applicant's signature. Then, you can prove that it's not your signature. If you tell the debt collector that you are a victim of identity theft and it is collecting the debt for another company, the debt collector must tell that company that you may be a victim of identity theft. While you can stop a debt collector from contacting you, that won't get rid of the debt itself.

It's important to contact the company that originally opened the account to dispute the debt, otherwise that company may send it to a different debt collector, report it on your credit report, or initiate a lawsuit to collect on the debt.

Mail Theft

The USPIS is the law enforcement arm of the U.S. Postal Service, and investigates cases of identity theft. The USPIS has primary jurisdiction in all matters infringing on the integrity of the U.S. mail.

If an identity thief has stolen your mail to get new credit cards, bank or credit card statements, pre-screened credit offers, or tax information, or has falsified change-of address forms or obtained your personal information through a fraud conducted by mail, report it to your local postal inspector. You will then want to get a post office box instead of having local delivery to protect your mail.

Phone Fraud

If an identity thief has established phone service in your name, is making unauthorized calls that seem to come from and are billed to your cellular phone, or is using your calling card and PIN, contact your service provider immediately to cancel the account and/or calling card. Open new accounts and choose new PIN numbers. Most companies will work with you to remove the fraudulent charges. If you're having trouble getting them removed from your account or getting an unauthorized account closed, contact the Federal Communications Commission. We have listed their contact info in the section under important numbers. You will, of course, also need to begin having your credit report corrected.

CHAPTER 5- HOW TO RE-ESTABLISH YOUR CREDIT SCORE

Your credit report contains information about where you live, how you pay your bills, and whether you've been sued, arrested, or filed for bankruptcy. Consumer reporting companies sell the information in your report to creditors, insurers, employers, and other businesses that use it to evaluate your applications for credit, insurance, employment, or renting a home.

The federal Fair Credit Reporting Act (FCRA) promotes the accuracy and privacy of information in the files of the nation's consumer reporting companies. In the case of identity theft and/or fraud, this step is essential in re-gaining your identity. Under the FCRA, both the consumer reporting company and the information provider (that is, the person, company, or organization that provides information about you to a consumer reporting company) are responsible for correcting inaccurate or incomplete information in your report.

To take advantage of all your rights under this law, contact the consumer reporting company and the information provider. Tell the consumer reporting company, in writing, what information you think is inaccurate. Include copies (NOT originals) of documents that support your position. This would include a copy of the police report you have filed. In addition to providing your complete name and address, your letter should clearly identify each item in your report you dispute, state the facts and explain why you dispute the information, and request that it be removed or corrected. You may want to enclose a copy of your report with the items in question circled. Send your letter by certified mail, "return receipt requested," so you can document what the consumer reporting company received. Keep copies of your dispute letter and enclosures.

Consumer reporting companies must investigate the items in question—usually within 30 days—unless they consider your dispute frivolous. They also must forward all the relevant data you provide about the inaccuracy to the organization that provided the information. After the information provider receives notice of a dispute from the consumer reporting company, it must investigate, review the relevant information, and report the results back to the consumer reporting company. If the information provider finds the disputed information is inaccurate, it must notify all three nationwide consumer reporting companies so they can correct the information in your file.

When the investigation is complete, the consumer reporting company must give you the results in writing and a free copy of your report if the dispute results in a change. This free report does not count as your annual free report. If an item is changed or deleted, the consumer reporting company cannot put the disputed information back in your file unless the information provider verifies that it is accurate and complete. The consumer reporting company also must send you written notice that includes the name, address, and phone number of the information provider. If you ask, the consumer reporting company must send notices of any corrections to anyone who received your report in the past six months. You can have a corrected copy of your report sent to anyone who received a copy during the past two years for employment purposes.

If an investigation doesn't resolve your dispute with the consumer reporting company, you can ask that a statement of the dispute be included in your file and in future reports. You also can ask the consumer reporting company to provide your statement to anyone who received a copy of your report in the recent past. You can expect to pay a fee for this service. You should also tell the creditor or other information provider, in writing, that you dispute an item. Be sure to include copies (NOT originals) of documents that support your position. Many providers specify an address for disputes. If the provider reports the item to a consumer reporting company, it must include a notice of your dispute. And if you are correct—that is, if the information is found to be inaccurate—the information provider may not report it again.

CHAPTER 6- SAMPLE DISPUTE LETTERS

For Credit Agencies

Date

Your Name

Your Address

Your City, State, Zip Code

Complaint Department

Name of Consumer Reporting Company

Address

City, State, Zip Code

Dear Sir or Madam:

I am a victim of identity theft. I am writing to request that you block the following fraudulent information in my file. This information does not relate to any transaction that I have made. The items also are circled on the attached copy of the report I received. (Identify item(s) to be blocked by name of source, such as creditors or tax court, and identify type of item, such as credit account, judgment, etc.).

Enclosed is a copy of the law enforcement report regarding my identity theft. Please let me know if you need any other information from me to block this information on my credit report.

Sincerely,

Your name

Enclosures: (List what you are enclosing.)

For Existing Accounts

Date

Your Name

Your Address

Your City, State, Zip Code

Your Account Number

Name of Creditor

Billing Inquiries

Address

City, State, Zip Code

Dear Sir or Madam:

I am writing to dispute a fraudulent (charge or debit) on my account in the amount of $_____$. I am a victim of identity theft, and I did not make this (charge or debit). I am requesting that the (charge be removed or the debit reinstated), that any finance and other charges related to the fraudulent amount be credited, as well, and that I receive an accurate statement.

Enclosed are copies of (use this sentence to describe any enclosed information, such as a police report) supporting my position. Please investigate this matter and correct the fraudulent (charge or debit) as soon as possible.

Don't Fall Victim to Identity Theft
Sincerely,

Your name

Enclosures: (List what you are enclosing.)

Identity Theft Affidavit

Name _____

Phone number _____

ID Theft Affidavit

Victim Information

My full legal name is

_____

(First) (Middle) (Last) (Jr., Sr., III)

(If different from above) When the events described in this affidavit took place, I was known as

_____

(First) (Middle) (Last) (Jr., Sr., III)

(3) My date of birth is _____ (Day/month/year)

(4) My Social Security number is _____

(5) My driver's license or identification card state and number are
_____

(6) My current address is

City _____ State _____ Zip Code _____

(7) I have lived at this address since _____ (Month/year)

(8) (If different from above) When the events described in this affidavit took place, my address was

_____

City _____ State _____ Zip Code _____

(9) I lived at the address in Item 8 from _____ until (month/year) _____ (month/year)

(10) My daytime telephone number is (____) _____

My evening telephone number is (____) _____

How the Fraud Occurred

Circle all that apply for items 11 - 17:

(11) I did not authorize anyone to use my name or personal information to seek the money, credit, loans, goods or services described in this report.

(12) I did not receive any benefit, money, goods or services as a result of the events described in this report.

(13) My identification documents (for example, credit cards; birth certificate; driver's license; Social Security card; etc.) were R stolen R lost on or about _____. (Day/month/year)

(14) To the best of my knowledge and belief, the following person(s) used my information (for example, my name, address, date of birth, existing account numbers, Social Security number, mother's maiden name, etc.) or identification documents to get money, credit, loans, goods or services without my knowledge or authorization:

Name (if known)

_____

Address (if known)

_____

Phone number(s) (if known)

_____

_____

Additional information (if known)

_____

Name (if known)

_____

Address (if known)

_____

Phone number(s) (if known)

_____

_____

Additional information (if known)

(15) I do NOT know who used my information or identification documents to get money, credit, loans, goods or services without my knowledge or authorization.

(16) Additional comments: (For example, description of the fraud, which documents or information was used or how the identity thief gained access to your information.)

_____

_____

_____

_____

_____

(Attach additional pages as necessary.)

Victim's Law Enforcement Actions

Circle One

(17) (I am) (am not) willing to assist in the prosecution of the person(s) who committed this fraud.

Circle One

(18) (I am) (am not) authorizing the release of this information to law enforcement for the purpose of assisting them in the investigation and prosecution of the person(s) who committed this fraud.

Circle One

(19) (I have) (have not) reported the events described in this affidavit to the police or other law enforcement agency.

The police (did) (did not) write a report. In the event you have contacted the police or other law enforcement agency, please complete the following:

_____

(Agency #1)

_____

(Officer/Agency personnel taking report)

_____

(Date of report)

_____

(Report number, if any)

_____

_____

(Phone number)

_____

(Email address, if any)

_____

Don't Fall Victim to Identity Theft
(Agency #2)

_____

(Officer/Agency personnel taking report)

_____

(Date of report)

_____

(Report number, if any)

_____

(Phone number)

_____

(Email address, if any)

Documentation Checklist

Please indicate the supporting documentation you are able to provide to the companies you plan to notify. Attach copies (NOT originals) to the affidavit before sending it to the companies.

(20) A copy of a valid government-issued photo identification card (for example, your driver's license, state issued ID card or your passport). If you are under 16 and don't have a photo-ID, you may submit a copy of your birth certificate or a copy of your official school records showing your enrollment and place of residence.

(21) Proof of residency during the time the disputed bill occurred, the loan was made or the other event took place (for example, a rental/lease agreement in your name, a copy of a utility bill or a copy of an insurance bill).

(22) A copy of the report you filed with the police or sheriff's department. If you are unable to obtain a report or report number from the police, please indicate that in Item

19. Some companies only need the report number, not a copy of the report. You may want to check with each company.

Signature

I certify that, to the best of my knowledge and belief, all the information on and attached to this affidavit is true, correct, and complete and made in good faith.

I also understand that is affidavit or the information it contains may be made available to federal, state, and/or local law enforcement agencies for such action within their jurisdiction as they deem appropriate.

I understand that knowingly making any false or fraudulent statement or representation to the government may constitute a violation of 18 U.S.C. §1001 or other federal, state, or local criminal statutes, and may result in imposition of a fine or imprisonment or both.

_____ (signature)

_____ (date signed)

_____ (Notary)

Don't Fall Victim to Identity Theft

[Check with each company. Creditors sometimes require notarization. If they do not, please have one witness (nonrelative) sign below that you completed and signed this affidavit.]

Witness:

_____

(Signature)

_____

(Printed name)

_____

(Date)

_____

(Telephone number)

It's a daunting process to be sure and one that will take quite some time to resolve, but it can be resolved. You can reclaim your identity! How do you prevent it from happening again?

CHAPTER 7- PROTECTING YOURSELF FROM IDENTITY THIEVES

When it comes to identity theft, you can't entirely control whether you will become a victim. But there are certain steps you can take to minimize recurrences. The first and possibly most important thing consumers can do to protect their identity is to monitor their credit reports. A recent amendment to the federal Fair Credit Reporting Act requires each of the major nationwide consumer reporting companies to provide you with a free copy of your credit reports, at your request, once every 12 months. To request a copy of your free credit report, call toll-free 1-877-322- 8228.

Do not contact the credit reporting companies directly. They only provide free reports through the above web address and phone number. If you notice anything wrong on your report, refer to the section on correcting your credit report to take the appropriate steps to have the information removed or amended. You will also want to investigate thoroughly your other financial accounts to be sure the problems don't extend to other areas. As we said earlier, be aware when billing statements don't arrive when they should, if you receive credit cards you didn't ask for, and if you've been denied credit for no apparent reason. These are all signs of identity theft.

Place passwords on your credit card, bank, and phone accounts. Avoid using easily available information like your mother's maiden name, your birth date, the last four digits of your SSN or your phone number, or a series of consecutive numbers. When opening new accounts, you may find that many businesses still have a line on their applications for your mother's maiden name. Ask if you can use a password instead. Secure personal information in your home, especially if you have roommates, employ outside help, or are having work done in your home. Consider using a post office box instead of home mail delivery to minimize the chances of mail theft.

Ask about information security procedures in your workplace or at businesses, doctor's offices or other institutions that collect your personally identifying information. Find out who has access to your personal information and verify that it is handled securely. Ask about the disposal procedures for those records as well. Find out if your information will be shared with anyone else. If so, ask how your information can be kept confidential.

If you are a member of the military and away from your usual duty station, you may place an active duty alert on your credit reports to help minimize the risk of identity theft while you are deployed. Active duty alerts are in effect on your report for one year. If your deployment lasts longer, you can place another alert on your credit report. When you place an active duty alert, you'll be removed from the credit reporting companies' marketing list for prescreened credit card offers for two years unless you ask to go back on the list before then. You can have an authorized agent do this for you, but make sure they have the proper authorization documentation to do so.

Don't give out personal information on the phone, through the mail, or on the Internet unless you've initiated the contact or are sure you know who you're dealing with. Identity thieves are clever, and have posed as representatives of banks, Internet service providers (ISPs), and even government agencies to get people to reveal their SSN, mother's maiden name, account numbers, and other identifying information. Before you share any personal information, confirm that you are dealing with a legitimate organization. Check an organization's website by typing its URL in the address line, rather than cutting and pasting it. Many companies post scam alerts when their name is used improperly. Or call customer service using the number listed on your account statement or in the telephone book.

Treat your mail and trash carefully. Deposit your outgoing mail in post office collection boxes or at your local post office, rather than in an unsecured mailbox. Promptly remove mail from your mailbox. If you're planning to be away from home and can't pick up your mail, contact your local Post Office to request a vacation hold. They will hold your mail there until you can pick it up or are home to receive it. To thwart an identity thief who may pick through your trash or recycling bins to capture your personal information, tear or shred your charge receipts, copies of credit applications, insurance forms, physician statements, checks and bank statements, expired charge cards that you're discarding, and credit offers you get in the mail. To opt out of receiving offers of credit in the mail, call: 1-888-5-OPTOUT (1-888-567-8688). You will be asked to provide your SSN which the consumer reporting companies need to match you with your file.

Don't carry your Social Security card with you; leave it in a secure place. Give your SSN only when absolutely necessary, and ask to use other types of identifiers. If your state uses your SSN as your driver's license number, ask to substitute another number. Do the same if your health insurance company uses your SSN as your policy number. Carry only the identification information and the credit and debit cards that you'll actually need when you go out. Keep your purse or wallet in a safe place at work; do the same with copies of administrative forms that have your sensitive personal information.

Be cautious when responding to promotions. Identity thieves may create phony promotional offers to get you to give them your personal information. I once had a co-worker who made copies of everything in his wallet once a month and kept them in a secure place inside his home. This is a great idea to easily help you keep track of credit cards (copy the front and back), checking account numbers, and health insurance information (again front and back copies).

When you use the ATM, be mindful of anyone around you. Cover the keypad when entering in your PIN to defeat prying eyes or miniature cameras. Do not allow yourself to be distracted when using the ATM. That is prime time for criminals to strike. You can physically protect yourself and your documents, but there are other ways for thieves to secure your personal operation – through your personal computer.

Chapter 8- Internet Security Tips for You and Your Family

When Downloading Attachments

It is very important to remember to be careful when you receive an email that comes with an attachment. It is doubly important if that attachment is from someone that you don't know.

As a rule, it is a good idea to delete the email and not even worry about it if it's from someone that you don't know and weren't expecting. After all, an email with an attachment can equate to a virus and a virus can harm your system so much that it might be beyond compare. In addition, you can lose valuable information and even have someone hack into your personal and financial information and use it for their own purposes.

It seems silly that people would waste their time trying to come up with different ways to destroy other people's systems, but it happens on a daily basis. Sometimes, people do it just because they can and there isn't reason a valid reason behind their actions.

This can be very frustrating for the victims of such an attack. You must learn to be cautious.

So how can you protect your internet security when it comes to downloading e-mail attachments?

Anti-virus software. You should definitely invest in some anti-virus software. This will scan the e-mails and attachments for you and let you know if they are safe. This can be particularly important if you are using free email accounts.

E-mail programs with built in sensors. If you pay for your e-mail account then chances are that it already has some sensors to detect harmful attachments. Sometimes, as soon as the e-mail itself comes in it is sent to the trash can or the harmful attachment itself is removed for safety precautions. This is ideal.

Ignore the mail. A lot of times people who send harmful things to your e-mail account try to get away with it by pretending that they know you or are sending you something that you already requested. Well, if you know them, then you should be able to identify the e-mail address. You should also recognize the name. Sometimes, they will use the name of a legitimate company to try to fool you. For example, it might say "Amazon" but when you look more closely at the e-mail address it might read amazon (at)hotmail (dot) com. Now, would it really make sense for Amazon to use a free e-mail account?

When Using Facebook

You probably have a Facebook account. If you don't, then chances are that your child does. Facebook can be an excellent way to interact with your friends and co-workers, as well as keep your family updated on what is going on in your life. You can post family vacation pictures, send emails, and "chat" with people that live far away. Better yet, you can do all of this for free! However, there are some risks associated with internet security when it comes to Facebook.

Luckily, Facebook is aware of these internet security risks. There are actually some things that you can do to help protect yourself. The following is a list of 5 tips that you can use to make sure that you are safe when using Facebook.

1. Make your profile private. You can do this in a number of ways. You can make it so that only your friends can see your information and photos, or you can make it so that people can see your name and information but not your photos or wall unless you add them as a friend. Check this out under your "privacy settings "tap on your account.

2. Block people that you don't want to see your information. There is a choice under their photograph that will allow you to block them. When you do this, you will not show up on a search that they do and they will not see anything having to do with your account. It will be as though you do not exist to this person. This is a good feature is someone specifically is bothering you.

3. Report cyber stalking or harassment. If you choose to block someone, a window will pop up asking you the reason. One of the choices is cyber stalking. Choose this option if it is true. It won't stop if people don't report it.

4. Only add people that you know. This will help your internet security tremendously. Having 300 or more friends just so that you can say you have a lot of them is not a good reason for continuing to add people.

5. Don't purchase anything via Facebook. Many applications cost money. Ignore these and use the multitude of free things that the site offers. You don't want your financial information to be compromised just because you send someone a picture of a birthday cake.

When Dating Online

A lot of people find great, healthy relationships through online dating communities. Most of the people who sign up for them are legitimately looking for love and relationships. However, there are always going to be people out there who will take advantage of others.

So what can you do to protect your internet security, and yourself, when using online dating websites?

1. If you do decide to meet someone in person, do it in a public place. Preferably, meet them in daylight hours and ask someone to go with you. If that doesn't work, then at least leave information with a trusted person which includes where you are going, how long you plan on staying, a s well as anything identifiable about the person that you are meeting.

2. Do not rely on a photograph. It might not even be the person that you are really talking to. Or, it could have been them 20 years before. People use different pictures or are dishonest about their appearance all the time.

3. Save all of your conversations in a file on your computer. Better yet, print them out. Keep them somewhere that is fairly easy to access.

4. Talking to someone online is not the same as talking to them in person. Don't rush the relationship and don't feel as though you have to meet them right away.

5. Use a different e-mail account for your online dating than you do for your regular emails.

6. Do not ever give out any personal information at the beginning. In addition, keep your last name and anything personal, such as your address and directions to your house private, until you have met the person and have gotten to know them a little bit better. If you must give them your number, give them a cell phone number instead of your house phone.

7. Find a reputable online dating service. Don't just go to Google and search for singles chat rooms. An account that you have to pay for is generally more reputable than one that is free of charge.

8. Don't post any racy or revealing photographs of yourself. This is sure to draw the wrong kind of person-and not one that is looking for a relationship with anything serious in mind. In addition, try to choose a screen name that isn't too revealing either.

When the Teens Are Using the Internet

There are a lot of safety risks out there for teens and tweens who use the Internet. However, this doesn't mean that they have to stop using the 'Net. Instead, they should use good judgment and try to make wise decisions. The following article lists some helpful tips to keep your teen and tween's internet security protected.

1. Don' let your username say too much about you. For instance, don't make it your name and age, like Susan16. Instead, make it something that doesn't say much about your name, age, or sex. Keep it as neutral and vague as possible.

2. Don't ever post your social security number, driver's license number, phone number, home address or credit card information on the internet. If a friend asks you for your number on Myspace then either email them a private message or wait until you see them in person.

3. Don't add friends on the Internet that you don't know. People often misrepresent themselves and pretend to be something they are not. It happens all the time and they are very good about it. Don't think that you will know the difference.

4. Never agree to meet someone in person that you have met off of the Internet. If you are part of a group and someone wants to get together to discuss something that sounds legitimate, have a parent go with you and meet in a public place. Never substitute a friend for a parent.

5. If you have concerns about someone who is harassing you on the Internet, tell an adult. Cyber stalking is being controlled these days and awareness is growing.

6. Make your profile private so that only the people you know can see your information and photos.

7. Do some research on sites before you sign up for them. Don't just join them because everyone else is. Learn how they work before you post anything.

8. Don't store your passwords on your computer. It can make hacking easier.

9. If you purchase something with a credit card, ensure that you are using a secure server. This should be noticeable by a little emblem on the bottom right hand side of your screen.

10. Consider not using your full name when you join a site. Not posting your last name is a great preventive measure when it comes to Internet security.

About The Author

Brian Lewis is a retired policeman who is well-versed with identity theft, having handled hundreds of such cases in the past. Having witnessed firsthand the struggles experienced by victims of identity theft, Brian has made it his personal mission to educate anyone who's willing to listen on the dangers of the crime.